First World War
and Army of Occupation
War Diary
France, Belgium and Germany

32 DIVISION
14 Infantry Brigade,
Brigade Trench Mortar Battery
8 August 1915 - 31 August 1916

WO95/2394/5

The Naval & Military Press Ltd
www.nmarchive.com
Published in association with The National Archives

Published by

The Naval & Military Press Ltd

Unit 10 Ridgewood Industrial Park,

Uckfield, East Sussex,

TN22 5QE England

Tel: +44 (0) 1825 749494

www.naval-military-press.com

www.nmarchive.com

This diary has been reprinted in facsimile from the original. Any imperfections are inevitably reproduced and the quality may fall short of modern type and cartographic standards.

© Crown Copyright
Images reproduced by permission of The National Archives, London, England, 2015.

Contents

Document type	Place/Title	Date From	Date To
Heading	WO95/2394 Aug '15-Aug '16 14 Inf Bde Trench Mortar Battery		
Heading	32nd Division 14th Infy Bde 14th Trench Mortar Bty 1915 Aug-Aug 1916		
War Diary	Trench. 134	08/08/1915	08/08/1915
War Diary	134 Trench	08/08/1915	15/08/1915
War Diary	134 Trench	11/08/1915	21/08/1915
War Diary	Chissalamour	21/08/1915	21/08/1915
War Diary	2nd Coy Infantry Brigade H.Q.	26/08/1915	26/08/1915
War Diary	Trench 134	20/09/1915	25/09/1915
War Diary	Trench 134 on Corps Pontage	25/09/1915	17/10/1915
War Diary	Trench 134	30/09/1915	03/10/1915
War Diary			
War Diary	Mortar Billet T 22 B.6.D.	21/11/1915	27/11/1915
War Diary	Mortar Billet T.22.C.21	17/11/1915	17/11/1915
War Diary	Mortar Billet	18/11/1915	20/11/1915
War Diary	Trench 134	16/11/1915	16/11/1915
War Diary	Mortar Billet T.22.d.42	31/10/1915	31/10/1915
War Diary	Mortar Billet	01/11/1915	03/11/1915
War Diary	Mortar Billet T.22.c.21.	07/11/1915	07/11/1915
War Diary	Mortar Billet	08/11/1915	13/11/1915
War Diary	Trench 134 A	03/11/1915	03/11/1915
War Diary	Mortar Billet	04/11/1915	06/11/1915
War Diary	Cleaning Billets Gill drill from 9 am till 11.am afternoon Wood Cleaning	29/11/1915	30/11/1915
War Diary	Marching drill Cleaning ref Billets	01/12/1915	01/12/1915
War Diary	Cleaning guys in advange Dugout & General Fatiques	02/12/1915	02/12/1915
War Diary	Lecture On Guns Cleaning Of Billets	03/12/1915	03/12/1915
War Diary	Marching drill & Fatigues	04/12/1915	04/12/1915
War Diary	Cleaning Of Billet	05/12/1915	05/12/1915
War Diary	14th TM Bty Billet	20/12/1915	25/12/1915
War Diary	Billet 22.C.52.	05/12/1915	11/12/1915
Miscellaneous	War Diary for the Week Ending December 18:15	18/12/1915	18/12/1915
War Diary	In the Field	26/12/1915	31/12/1915
Heading	14th Brigade. 32nd Division. 14th Trench Mortar Battery July 1916		
War Diary	Authville	01/07/1916	03/07/1916
War Diary	Leipsig Salient	04/07/1916	04/07/1916
War Diary	Senlis	05/07/1916	05/07/1916
War Diary	Forleville	06/07/1916	07/07/1916
War Diary	Bouzincourt	08/07/1916	08/07/1916
War Diary	Ovillers	09/07/1916	12/07/1916
War Diary	Bouzincourt	13/07/1916	15/07/1916
War Diary	Warloy	16/07/1916	16/07/1916
War Diary	Beauval	17/07/1916	17/07/1916
War Diary	Le Souich	18/07/1916	19/07/1916
War Diary	Monts-En-Ternois	20/07/1916	20/07/1916
War Diary	Monchy-Breton	21/07/1916	21/07/1916
War Diary	Cauchy-A-La-Tour	22/07/1916	26/07/1916
War Diary	Ruitz	27/07/1916	29/07/1916

Heading	14th Brigade. 32nd Division. 14th Trench Mortar Battery August 1916		
War Diary	Annezin-Les-Bethune	30/07/1916	31/07/1916
War Diary	Annezin	01/08/1916	04/08/1916
War Diary	Le Preol	05/08/1916	05/08/1916
War Diary	Cuinchy	06/08/1916	31/08/1916
Miscellaneous	2 (a) Appendix B.1.		

WO95/2394

Aug '15 - Aug '16

14 INF BDE
 — TRENCH MORTAR BATTERY

32ND DIVISION
14TH INFY BDE

14TH TRENCH MORTAR BTY

1915 AUG - AUG 1916

32ND DIVISION
14TH INFY BDE

Army Form C. 2118

WAR DIARY
or
INTELLIGENCE SUMMARY.
(Erase heading not required.)

Instructions regarding War Diaries and Intelligence Summaries are contained in F.S. Regs., Part II. and the Staff Manual respectively. Title pages will be prepared in manuscript.

Hour, Date, Place	Summary of Events and Information	Remarks and references to Appendices
8.8.15. 4.30. P.M. Trench 134.	1915 Nothing to report. Battery strength. 2. Officers. 1. Sergt. 3. C.pls. 1. Bdr. 17. Gunners.	

(B 29 6) W 4141—463 100,000 9/14 H W V Forms/C. 2118/10

WAR DIARY
or
INTELLIGENCE SUMMARY.
(Erase heading not required.)

Army Form C. 2118.

Hour, Date, Place	Summary of Events and Information	Remarks and references to Appendices
2.30 - 3.30 a.m. 8th August. 134 Trench.	Germans threw over several Rifle Grenades & trench Mortars from La Plus Douve Farm (Sheet 28, Belgium & France B Series. S.W. 2nd Edition uncoloured, U.8.A.9.6) Several launched short. Only one or two hitting the trench. We did not retaliate owing to scarcity of Mud or Ammunition.	20,000
3.30 a.m. 15th August. 134 Trench.	Machine gun in La Plus Douve Farm (German) was fired on by No.1 A.S.A. Colt Trench Mor. One burst hit the mouth, but failed to explode. The second ranching to little too much to the left	U.8.A.9.6)
Wednesday 11th — 15th August.	German Artillery have been very active every afternoon from Wednesday on, and have been putting over some very heavy shells, you cannot hear this report of their guns, even with the wind in your favour, and you can distinctly hear the Burst of the shell for about 7 secs (timed by W/Watch) after the shell had passed over head. They were firing on Neuve Eglise about 4 miles back.	All places in this paper come into 12 —— Sheet. Belgium & France Sheet 28 Series South West 2nd Edition uncoloured 20,000 La Plus Douve Farm = U.8.A.9.6

Army Form C. 2118

WAR DIARY
or
INTELLIGENCE SUMMARY.
(Erase heading not required.)

Instructions regarding War Diaries and Intelligence Summaries are contained in F. S. Regs., Part II. and the Staff Manual respectively. Title pages will be prepared in manuscript.

H.Q. 1st Canadian Hy. B'y

Hour, Date, Place	Summary of Events and Information	Remarks and references to Appendices
4 A.M. – 4.30 A.M. 18th Aug. T.134	We fired 3 Trench Mortars observing considerable damage to machine gun emplacement in Plus Douve farm. The Germans retaliated with about 20 Trench Mortars, doing no damage, & only slightly wounding one man in the trench.	
3 P.M. – 4 P.M. 18th Aug. T.134.	We were fired upon from behind with 4.2" guns. The first 4 shots were direct on. Disarranged. Then 2 fell short just in front of our wire & failed to explode. But of the remaining 4 shots, 2 fell in their wire & 2 just over the ditch, hitting the farm wall, and knocking a considerable portion down.	
3.30 – 5 A.M. 21st August. Trench 134.	Our Trench Mortars opened fire on a concrete Machine gun emplacement of the Germans in the trench just in front of Le Plus Douve farm. The enemy was let after the 2nd shell. Germans retaliated with several Trench Mortars and rifle grenades also a field gun period on our trenches with shrapnel. Our Artillery retaliated as well as Trench Mortars & succeeded in putting two Trench Mortars out of action.	19/8/15
6.10 P.M. 21st August.	A large explosion followed by rapid fire and firing of German guns from Messines Hill took place in our left. It lasted for about 15 minutes. Unofficial report states that we put up a mine.	
Wuslakenen.	Germans put up a white flag in their work on the right of the 20.21st Gr.O. The 13th Bn. Canadians brought it in. But it was written — We have captured 85,000 Russian prisoners, & several 2000 Guns.	H.Q. Muston on the Sir. Q.E. N.M. Trench Howitzer Batt

Forms/C. 2118/10

Army Form C. 2118.

WAR DIARY
or
INTELLIGENCE SUMMARY.
(Erase heading not required.)

1st Hy. [Trench?] Mortar Bty.

Hour, Date, Place	Summary of Events and Information	Remarks and references to Appendices
10.55 P.M. Reg[imenta]l depot 3rd Heavy [illegible] H.Q.	At 10.55 P.M. news [illegible] was big [illegible] seen in the register of our trenches at 3700 y 21 as [illegible] and up the [illegible] of two [illegible] this could not [illegible] so [illegible] of men [illegible] a [illegible] rarely [illegible] and [illegible] figure in a most [illegible] direction at 3700	

10/21/15

[illegible signature]
O.C. 1st Heavy Mortar Battery

WAR DIARY
or
INTELLIGENCE SUMMARY.
(Erase heading not required.)

Army Form C. 2118

Instructions regarding War Diaries and Intelligence Summaries are contained in F.S. Regs., Part II. and the Staff Manual respectively. Title pages will be prepared in manuscript.

Hour, Date, Place	Summary of Events and Information	Remarks and references to Appendices

3 a.m. 30 Sept 1914
Trench 13a

8 p.m. 24th 46a & 23b

Ordered to open fire at 3 A.M. Diverged. This was about clearing stores of dark & & owing to noise of the enemy during the day was a considerable & at 3.20 & 3.30 Sept 1915.

Shooting 4 gun salvos + a second at object near 13s 4 double salvos per 7 rounds. It was reported much at the woods by officer. There rifles at 6 p.m. we had A shot from the ground artillery of one of 100 rounds at Gomain fuses on The whole can at everyone. This occurred with scattered rounds as far as the evening. Spre into the shooting about 30 rounds was fired into two traverse gun emplacement at one of 220. 633 + 229 6 9.3. We remembered the wheel & fell in the ocean. The enemy thus did not reach our own positions tired by us, but fired on the Germans on The North way. All guns which [illegible] [illegible] & [illegible] [illegible].

Ammunition: There were no casualties.

WAR DIARY or INTELLIGENCE SUMMARY

Army Form C. 2118

14th ?? French Mortar Bty?

Hour, Date, Place	Summary of Events and Information	Remarks and references to Appendices
2.p.m. 25th Trench 134 y or Loop fosage.	At 2 p.m. our Howitzers opened on Trenches on the ridge to our left. The Germans took about an hour to retaliate and instead of retaliating on the right retaliated on Mortar position & flagpoles trenches in rear of 134. The Germans sent over salvo after salvo of high explosives of 150# many heavy shrap must have burst as well. Their Trench Mortars stopped to bombard our front & at no ??? fired from this position, it was not until 6 fire upon the position openly, no opposition was ready for defence proposed. The Germans ceased retaliation at dusk.	1.20/10
6 p.m. 16/10/15	Battery was asked to give an retaliation to German Trench Mortars. Ten rounds were fired on their front line trench to west east of Petit Bois as a ??? Eight rounds fired in retaliation	It was reported by the O.C. 7th ?? that such was very good.
2.15 am 17/10/15	do.	
11.40 am 17/10/15	do.	
	The German sent Rabaris fired at intervals of 10 to 15 minutes in a few rounds burst in angle 16/17/10/15 indently searching for our Mortar emplacement	W H Smithson Lt O C 14th French Mortar Bty 13th ??

Army Form C. 2118

14 French Mortar Bty

WAR DIARY
or
INTELLIGENCE SUMMARY.
(Erase heading not required.)

Instructions regarding War Diaries and Intelligence Summaries are contained in F.S. Regs., Part II. and the Staff Manual respectively. Title pages will be prepared in manuscript.

Hour, Date, Place	Summary of Events and Information	Remarks and references to Appendices
8.50 P.m. 30th September Trench 13 a	The Germans opened fire on our front trench with Trench Mortars & rifle grenades, we retaliated with great effect on their trenches and every one of their mortars which we sent down the spotted fire at dawn & we had to cease firing	
1st Oct. 1.30 a.m – 2 p.m Trench 13 a	Germans opened fire at 12 a.m. and replied immediately but did not cease fire till about 2 a.m. we retaliated with bos from the two mortars & fair shore [illegible] did not remove enough ammunition for 2nd mortar	
2nd Oct. – 2 p.m. Trench 13 a	Germans opened fire & sent over a few shells & crumps so [illegible] had time but retaliated 30 from two trenches & got answer back in a while when we attack the aeroplane, was noticed that bomb-fired the one was fired we are specially the one Lieut Col odd sent right into the German trenches, but managed to put two Mortars out of action and every rifleman [illegible]	
3rd Oct. 2 a.m – 5 a.m	The Germans were very hostile starting off with a burst of heavy artillery fire & then answering with Trench Mortars. Our had to ask on artillery day to ceasing & fire T takes where	

(9 29 6) W 4141-463 100,000 9/14 H W V Forms/C. 2118/10

Army Form C. 2118.

WAR DIARY
or
INTELLIGENCE SUMMARY.
(Erase heading not required.)

Instructions regarding War Diaries and Intelligence Summaries are contained in F.S. Regs., Part II. and the Staff Manual respectively. Title pages will be prepared in manuscript.

Hour, Date, Place	Summary of Events and Information	Remarks and references to Appendices
	1st Nov. Ouderdom. There I have been not rumours from HQ the batlfront of at 5.30 PM. the Germans fought up to 15 trench Mortars not being used by very bad shooting. No percussion action, between our lines & the Germans. It is intended at 75° angle for the projectors of 134-135.	
	[signed] H.M.H. Godstone Lt. O.C. No 14 Trench Mortar Battery	

14th Gwent Mitn Bn Bly

"B" 29 "

Army Form C. 2118

WAR DIARY
INTELLIGENCE SUMMARY.
(Erase heading not required.)

Instructions regarding War Diaries and Intelligence Summaries are contained in F. S. Regs., Part II. and the Staff Manual respectively. Title pages will be prepared in manuscript.

Hour, Date, Place	Summary of Events and Information	Remarks and references to Appendices
10 A.m. 21.11.15 Morton Billet T2 2 B.6.0.	Parade. Gen Drill. 2.30. Lecture Drill	
11 A.m. 22.11.15 Do	Route March.	
10 A.m. 23.11.15 Do	Kit Inspection. 2.30. lecture on Ammunition	
10 A.m. 24.11.15 Do	Battery proceeded to Cane bes to take guns back to Stores yards, owing to no Ammunition & Wagons.	
10 A.m. 25.11.15 Do	Gun Drill & section drill. Lecture on equipment of general appearance.	
10 A.m. 26.11.15 Do	Cleaning guns & tents. 2.30. Squad drill.	
15 A.m. 27.11.15 Do	Inspection of Billets & huts	

H A Hill Lt
OC 14/H French mortar Battn
27.11.15

Forms/C. 2118/10

14th Trench Mortar Battery

WAR DIARY or INTELLIGENCE SUMMARY

Hour, Date, Place	Summary of Events and Information	Remarks and references to Appendices
17th Inst. Motor Relief T.2.C.2.1.	Nine Army Australians or Bavarians. It was doubted the Germans had fired their 3rd Red Rocket & that infantry had rushed our trenches in reply, had the Germans done this. Moved about 3 A.m. Dm. Corporal McKenzie & Pte Hughes both	
18th " Motor Relief	5th Dec. Enclaimed myself was trying to get the gun & the tool & the support line. The first shell landed on O more than 20y from us & it was with great energy that Corporal McKenzie & Pte	
19th Inst " "	they succeeded in reaching the dug out line, & clearing the gun. The Germs had the line in 9 O.C over the S.m. as all communication trenches were full of water or mud. The Battery returned to their Billets at 5 A.m. on the 17th Inst.	
20th Inst motor Relief	The men were given the day to get cleaned up & dry. It was reported that as 8 of our aeroplanes had been seen & fell near the front line.	
	10 A.m. Kit Inspection. 2.30. Gun drill. Parade 9.30 – 11.30. Relieve beds and bields	
	12 n.d. Battery proceeded to Trenches, but were returned to their own billet for attending & doing Preconcertion	

H.M.Wo[?] unbrother Lt
E.C. No 14 Trench Motor Battery
20.11.15.

WAR DIARY or INTELLIGENCE SUMMARY

Army Form C. 2118.

Hour, Date, Place	Summary of Events and Information	Remarks and references to Appendices
5 P.m. 13th Inst. Trench 134.	The Battery proceeded to the trenches at 5 P.m. and placed the guns in Prior Farm, which is just behind the support trenches & owing to all our dugouts having been either washed away or demolished by shell fire or fallen in on account of the rain, the Officers & men had no where to sleep, 10 had to spend the night in the open.	
14th Inst. Trench 134.	Acting Capt. Toyford Wallace 8th Bn Canadians owing to sickness on the night of the 13th Inst reported sick at Hospital with Neuralgia at 6 P.m. The guns were taken into position in the front line bay. During 24 rounds of G.E.P. only two fuse noses (when at Staltenbergs) owing to there being no accommodation in the front line, one life guard on the guns & sent the men to a cellar which they had found in a ruined house at Rong iel.	
15th Inst. 5 P.m. Trench 134.	Trench mortars registered on Petit Dona Farm from new positions. The first shot landing in enemy's trench. On firing 3 shots from second position none went off. Evidently some damage had been done to enemy and sent over 12 small 10 lb messenger and heavy. Part 4.1" shells. 7 of the shells failed to explode on hed. The shells which also exploded landed in the trenches or at fair out of toto and blew it to pieces; also, 3 pickets & spread bars. No fuses were ever found.	

Forms/C. 2118/10
(9 29 6) W4141—463 100,000 9/14 HWV

WAR DIARY or INTELLIGENCE SUMMARY

Army Form C. 2118.

Instructions regarding War Diaries and Intelligence Summaries are contained in F.S. Regs., Part II. and the Staff Manual respectively. Title pages will be prepared in manuscript.

(Erase heading not required.)

Hour, Date, Place	Summary of Events and Information	Remarks and references to Appendices
2.B. 16th Bn St. T. Trench 134.	The enemy bombed, burnt & spent shrapnel had been let in up without interference of our trenches so we were able to carry on with our work. The other was removed to Irish farm. The Germans started registering on T.134 and landed 30 shells round about our No 2 gun position. 20 of the shells failed to explode. The gun position was changed. Our 6" 4.5" did some excellent work on the enemy's trenches also the 12" which was firing on Messines. At the stroke of every hour from 5 PM till 2 Am the French Mortar fired 1 bomb. This was done to keep down enemy working parties & to give the enemy plenty of work to do in another sector to the same on side the T.P.R. Casualties were 0 & 5. During the 10 rounds exploded it was checked to keep the enemy & bombs till 2.25 Am just before the attack was launched and to fire in conjunction with machine guns. The last 8 were very successful landing either in the trenches or just behind will allow our own men making enough noise & disturbance to allow our [?] of the 7th K.O. Bn. to get through the wire. At 2.30 Am the 7th Bn Bombers entered the enemies trench. They took 12 prisoners. 3 of which were [Prussians?]	

WAR DIARY
or
INTELLIGENCE SUMMARY

Army Form C. 2118

14th Imperial Mountain Battery

Hour, Date, Place	Summary of Events and Information	Remarks and references to Appendices
3. 9 P.m. 31st October. Mata Billet. T.22.a.42.	Owing to so many miss fires and to many bombs not exploding, it was decided to test them before the 2nd Brigade left, but if the 1st 12 that were fired 11 failed to explode. On consulting with the Bde. we decided to fire 8 more. None of these went off. Up to this time we had 12 misfires with T. Tubes. On firing another 8 bombs four of them exploded. There were a lot of different fuses, some were marked 2, 4, 6, 7. N° 2.4.6. failed. Of 47 very Time Maroli 7 was the only one to explode. As the result of the bombs that did go off we had 3 direct hits. The other 5 exploding in the air.	
9 A.m. 1st November. Mata Billet	Gun detail was carried out till 11.30 A.M. Owing to Rain the drill was stopped at 11.30 A.M. At 2.30. Gun detail was carried on for 1 hour. At 8 P.m. we received some 33 lb bombs from the D.A.C.	1. 31/10/15
9 A.m. 2nd November. Mata Billet	On examining the fuses they were exactly the same as the last we were having 3 cuts 3 as well. 6 of these bombs were tested. 4 of Duds failed to explode. Another 3 were tried. One failed to explode. At 4 P.m. One gun position in the Trenches was examined. Both the dug outs started to leak and at a little later collapsed. It is proposed of this room dug on and the Water Valley floods, to construct a raft capable of holding and firing a 1.6" Trench Mortar.	
9 A.m. 3rd November. Bar Tar Billet	Repairing damage of S.W.G line falling in shell holes. Kit Inspection took place at 2.30 P.m. The Battery proceeded to the Trench at 6 P.m. to repair damage done to fire positions by water and shells. Also to repair Dug outs.	

Army Form C. 2118

14th Trench Mortar Bty

WAR DIARY
or
INTELLIGENCE SUMMARY.
(Erase heading not required.)

Instructions regarding War Diaries and Intelligence Summaries are contained in F.S. Regs., Part II. and the Staff Manual respectively. Title pages will be prepared in manuscript.

Hour, Date, Place	Summary of Events and Information	Remarks and references to Appendices
2.P.M. Sunday 7th Mortar Billet T.22.C.21.	Battery paraded and proceeded to the Trenches to rebuild dug outs. On arriving there both dug out had fallen in owing to the rain.	Mortar Billet is T.22.c.21 sheet 28 B. near Belgium & France.
10.P.M. Monday 8th Mortar Billet	Gun Drill till 11.30. Lecture on positions of the team up in case of attack or defence. At 2.30 - 3.30 squad drill. Owing to the damp no helps taking place in the Trenches no work could be done & the dug outs.	
10.A.M. Tuesday 9th Mortar Billet.	Gun Drill till 11.30. 3.0 P.M. Battery paraded & Trenches for more work on dug outs. Returning at 11 P.M.	
12.P.M. Wednesday 10th M.B.	No parade this morning owing to men chopping & cleaning their clothing. 12. N.N. Parade & proceeded to Trenches to complete dug outs.	
9.30 A.M. Thursday 11th M.B.	Gun drill till 11.A.M. 2.P.M. Kit Inspection. Owing to rain the Battery were not able to proceed to Trenches.	
9.30 A.M. Friday. 12th M.B.	Lecture on favorable position to take up in case of advance or retreat. 2.P.M. Examination on Trench Mortars (British made.)	H 14/11/15
10.A.M. Saturday 13th M.B.	Cleaning Billets & Tents. 5.P.M. Battery proceeded to the Trenches.	

H.O.H. Gabathan
O.C. No. 14 Trench Mortar Battery
13th November 1915

Army Form C. 2118.

WAR DIARY
INTELLIGENCE SUMMARY.
(Erase heading not required.)

Instructions regarding War Diaries and Intelligence Summaries are contained in F. S. Regs., Part II. and the Staff Manual respectively. Title pages will be prepared in manuscript.

Hour, Date, Place	Summary of Events and Information	Remarks and references to Appendices
7 P.M. 3rd November Trench 134 A.	Owing to the element of work entailed in removing guns the duty was not able to be finished. All possible positions for mortars in the front line in the Richter Defence position are under about 4 ft of water. There is only one possible position left and if any heart of guns. However it is to be made into a position for the Battery. Sapper Williams was wounded through both legs while taking a gun out. The Battery had to take guns over the ground as the communication trenches are about full of water. Work was stopped at 1 A.M. Owing soon two men fell into the Dover river and nearly got drowned. Various fester parts and pegs have been washed away in the last 24 hrs.	
9 A.M. 4th November Mortar Billet	The guns were cleaned this morning. The remainder of the day was taken up with trying to get the mens clothes dry as all were very dirty after last nights work. At 3 P.M. the Battery had rifle shooting making some very good appeloate. ½ Butt at 40 yds.	
9.30 A.M. 5th Nov. Mortar Billet	Gun drill & squad drill 9.30 - 12 A.M. Parade at 2 P.M. lecture on fuses and ammunition.	
9.30 A.M. 6th Nov. Mortar Billet	Silvering of guns and Billet grounds. 11 A.M. Inspection of same.	

H. Hyndston Lt.
O C N 6/1st Trench Mortar Battery
For week ending 6th November 1915.

Army Form C. 2118.

WAR DIARY
or
INTELLIGENCE SUMMARY.

(Erase heading not required.)

Instructions regarding War Diaries and Intelligence Summaries are contained in F. S. Regs., Part II. and the Staff Manual respectively. Title pages will be prepared in manuscript.

Hour, Date, Place	Summary of Events and Information	Remarks and references to Appendices
Oct 11. 1915. Cleaning Billets. Gun Drill from 9am till 9.am Afternoon coin fatigue.		
1st Marching drill, cleaning up Billets.	Nil	
2nd Cleaning guns in advance Dugout's. General Fatigues.		
3rd Stables or guns & cleaning up Billets.		
4th Marching drill & Fatigues.	Nil	
5th Cleaning up Billets.		

A. McPherson LtCol
Cmdg T.M. Batteries
1 Canadian Division

N. Heffier Major
For O.C. H.T. 843

Army Form C. 2118

WAR DIARY
or
INTELLIGENCE SUMMARY
(Erase heading not required.)

Place	Date Dec	Hour	Summary of Events and Information	Remarks and references to Appendices
14th TM Bty Billets	20th		Cleaning Guns & Fatigues	
	21		Cleaning up billets	
	22		Cleaning up billets for inspection by O.C., T.M. Batteries. Right half Battery proceeded to trenches at 2 pm fired two rounds & had to retire owing to heavy shell fire	
	23		Right Half Shelled on way to gun emplacement & did not fire owing to rain. Left Half Cleaning billets & fatigues	
	24		Right Half Chose position in 55 Bn area No firing. Left Half Fatigues & cleaning billets	
	25		Right Half No firing Left Half Fatigues (Xmas Day)	

G.H.Butt 2nd Lt 14th T.M. Bty.
To O.C. T.M. Batteries
1st Can Div.

Army Form C. 2118

WAR DIARY
or
INTELLIGENCE SUMMARY.
(Erase heading not required.)

Instructions regarding War Diaries and Intelligence Summaries are contained in F. S. Regs., Part II. and the Staff Manual respectively. Title pages will be prepared in manuscript.

Hour, Date, Place	Summary of Events and Information	Remarks and references to Appendices
Billet 20.6.S.L.		
Sunday 5th 1915	Cleaning up Billets	
Monday 6th "	Gun Drill from 9 am till 11 am.	
Tuesday 7th "	Cleaning Guns in Advance Billet. Fatigues Form	
Wednesday 8th "	9 am till 10.30 am. Cleaning Guns from 9 am till 10 am. Afternoon Battle	
Thursday 9th "	Cleaning up Billets & wood Fatigue from 9 am till 11 am.	
Friday 10th "	Cleaning Guns & Fatigues from 9 am till 11 am.	
Saturday 11th "	Cleaning up Billet & Guns from 9 am till 11 am.	

G.F.Butt 2/Lt.

A.F.[...] Commanding
14th Trench Mortar Battery

14th Trench Mortar Battery

War diary for the week ending December 18th/15

December 12th 1915; Cleaning up Billets & Guns.

December 13th. Gun drill & Fatigues.

December 14th. Bombarding Barricade & Fatigues

December 15th. Cleaning Guns & Fatigues.

December 16th. Removing Gun & bombs from trenches to Irish Farm.

December 17th. Cleaning up Billets & Fatigues.

December 18th. Cleaning up billets & wood Fatigues

H Higginbotham
O.C. No 14 Trench Mortar Battery

18.12.15

Officer Commanding
14th Trench Mortar Battery

Army Form. C. 2118

14th Trench Mortar Batty
1st Can Div

WAR DIARY
or
INTELLIGENCE SUMMARY
(Erase heading not required.)

Instructions regarding War Diaries and Intelligence Summaries are contained in F. S. Regs., Part II. and the Staff Manual respectively. Title Pages will be prepared in manuscript.

Place	Date	Hour	Summary of Events and Information	Remarks and references to Appendices
In Field	26		Right half Battery in trenches. No rounds fired.	
			Left " " " " Fatigues	
	27		Right " " in trenches. Two rounds fired. 60 prs.	
			Left " " Cleaning billets	
	28		Right " " returned from trenches	
			Left " " relieved right half in trenches. No firing.	
	29		Right " " Cleaning billets. Firing & fatigues	
			Left " " No rounds fired	
	30		Right " " Cleaning billets & fatigues	
			Left " " No rounds fired.	
	31		Right " " Holidays	
			Left " " No firing	
	1		Right " " Cleaning, firing & Pde, fatigues	
			Left " " No firing.	

G.B. Butt 2/Lt
14th T.M. Battery

3/1/16
14th T.M. Battery

14th Brigade.

32nd Division.

14th TRENCH MORTAR BATTERY

JULY 1 9 1 6

WAR DIARY or INTELLIGENCE SUMMARY

(Erase heading not required.)

14th French Mortar Battery.

Army Form C. 2118

Place	Date	Hour	Summary of Events and Information	Remarks and references to Appendices
AUTHUILLE	July 1st	7.30am	For attack with infantry, Battery divided into 3 sections of 4 guns each. No 1 behind 1st Coy. of 1st DORSET REG'T., No 2 with 2nd MANCHESTER REG'T. No 3 in reserve. Infantry did not gain objective and No 1 Section could not get into action owing to heavy machine gun fire. 2nd Lieut. H.L. McINTYRE in charge of No 1 was killed by shell in front of my line. Gun teams and ammunition heavy casualties.	
		10.0am	No 2 section did not go forward owing to change of plan of infantry. Remained in AUTHUILLE WOOD.	R.C.S.
			No 3 Section in assembly trenches in AUTHUILLE WOOD. Heavily shelled. Weather fine.	
"	2nd		Battery reassembled in AUTHUILLE WOOD. Continuous shelling especially with lacrymatory shells. 2nd Lieut. R.L. GEORGE joined for duty.	R.C.S.
"	3rd		Shelling of wood increased. A steady rain made lacrymation shells more effective causing suffering & discomfort to troops. 6 pm. 2 guns (Lieut. PECK & 2/Lieut. DAME) taken into LEIPSIG SALIENT. Casualties infantry in repelling bombing attacks, from ill wind and water. Adverse conditions, no cover; trenches full of mud and water.	R.C.S.
LEIPSIG SALIENT	4th	12 noon	Repeated bombing by both sides. Suppressed by our guns. Culminated in heavy enemy counter attack about 12 noon during thunderstorm. This was repulsed.	R.C.S.
		5 pm	No. of rounds fired since 6 pm previous day = 200. Relieved by 4th BRIGADE.	R.C.S.
		11 pm	Gunners in billets at SENLIS.	R.C.S.

Army Form C. 2118

WAR DIARY
or
INTELLIGENCE SUMMARY
(Erase heading not required.)

14th Trench Mortar Battery

Instructions regarding War Diaries and Intelligence Summaries are contained in F.S. Regs., Part II. and the Staff Manual respectively. Title Pages will be prepared in manuscript.

Place	Date	Hour	Summary of Events and Information	Remarks and references to Appendices
SENLIS	July 5th	3pm	Brigade moved to FORCEVILLE	R.L.G.
FORCEVILLE	6th		The whole day - Rest in billets. Weather overcast.	R.L.G.
"	7th	11am	Returned to SENLIS & later proceeded to BOUZINCOURT. Conditions deplorable.	R.L.G.
BOUZINCOURT	8th		The dugout returned to the line in the OUILLERS sector. 2 guns were taken who him in position by midnight. Rats & additional guns in position. Head of guns were placed 20 in either flank of our position in village.	R.L.G.
OUILLERS	9th		Guns carried in emergency trenches behind their trouting parts. Close cooperation with infantry. 2nd MANCHESTER REGT. and 2nd Batterman avoided supported by us. Great activity on both sides during the night. Enemy artillery searched for our guns but did no damage.	R.L.G.
"	10th	9pm	Enemy maintained the present Rys bay. Attack left by 2nd INNISKILLING FUS. was supported by my guns with good effect.	R.L.G.
"	11th		Left our woods to give close support to INNIS. FUS. in new position. Superiority of fire established. Enemy trench and rifle grenade two mortars. Heavy expenditure of ammunition - about 600 rounds during 3 days.	R.L.G.
"	12th		Relieved by the 96th BRIGADE T.M.B. at 12 noon. Rejoined 14th BRIGADE at BOUZINCOURT. Austerity 5-9 killed 2 men wounded. 5 O.R. at CRUCIFIX CORNER when relief had been completed.	R.L.G.
BOUZINCOURT	13th		6 O.R. from 1st DORSET REGT. and 6 O.R. from 2nd MANCHESTER REGT. attached to Battery	R.L.G.

Army Form C. 2118

WAR DIARY
or
INTELLIGENCE SUMMARY
(Erase heading not required.)

14th T.M. Bn Hy.

Instructions regarding War Diaries and Intelligence Summaries are contained in F. S. Regs., Part II. and the Staff Manual respectively. Title Pages will be prepared in manuscript.

Place	Date	Hour	Summary of Events and Information	Remarks and references to Appendices
BERGUENEUSE	14-7-16		Held in readiness to return to the line. 2/Lieut. J. WALKER 15th H.L.I. joined for duty.	R.L.9.
"	15-7-16		Orders to go into trenches cancelled. Proceeded with Brigade to WARLOY-BAILLON. Weather fine.	R.L.9.
WARLOY	16-7-16		Marched remainder of the Brigade to BEAUVAL (18 Km.). Very hot.	R.L.9.
BEAUVAL	17-7-16		Marched to LE SOUICH where we came directly under orders of 14th BRIGADE.	R.L.9.
LE SOUICH	18-7-16		Rested in Billets. Weather cloudy.	R.L.9.
"	19-7-16		Marched with Brigade to MONTS-EN-TERNOIS	R.L.9.
MONTS-EN-TERNOIS	20-7-16		Marched to MONCHY-BRETON. Handcart in a long march proved an encumbrance. Very hot	R.C.9.
MONCHY-BRETON	21-7-16		Marched to CAUCHY-A-LA-TOUR.	R.L.9.
CAUCHY-A-LA-TOUR	22-7-16		Rested in Billets. 19th LAN.FUS.	R.L.9.
"	23-7-16		Inspection kit etc. Baths. 2/Lieut. L.B. MIDGLEY joined for duty.	R.L.9.
"	24-7-16		Class for attached men. 2/Lieut. G.H. DAWE proceeded to Divisional School as Instructor.	R.L.9.
"	25-7-16		" in Billets	R.L.9.
"	26-7-16		Marched under Brigade to RUITZ.	R.L.9.
RUITZ	27-7-16	9.30am	Inspected by G.O.C. 14th Brigade.	R.L.9.
"	28-7-16	3.0pm	Inspected by G.O.C. 1st Army. Lieut. E.K.B. PECK admitted to hospital	R.L.9.
"	29-7-16		Marched to ANNEZIN-LES-BETHUNE.	R.L.9.

14th Brigade.

32nd Division.

14th TRENCH MORTAR BATTERY

AUGUST 1 9 1 6

WAR DIARY
or
INTELLIGENCE SUMMARY

(Erase heading not required.)

14th T.M. Battery

Place	Date	Hour	Summary of Events and Information	Remarks and references to Appendices
ANNEZIN-LES-BETHUNE	30-7-16		In Billets. 2/Lieut. H.W. HANNAH 5th Royal Scots joined for duty vice 2/Lieut. WALKER	R.L.E.
— " —	31-7-16		Programme of training approved by Division entered upon.	R.L.S.

R.L. George
2/Lieut.
O.C. 14th T.M. Battery.

WAR DIARY or INTELLIGENCE SUMMARY

(Erase heading not required.)

14th K. T.M. Battery

Place	Date	Hour	Summary of Events and Information	Remarks and references to Appendices
ANNEZIN	1.8.16		Training as per programme. Special instructions for attached N.C.O.s and men.	R.K.9.
"	2.8.16		As previous day.	R.K.9.
"	3.8.16		ditto	R.K.9.
"	4.8.16	2.30pm	Battery marched to Bivouac at F.10.c. Central near LE PREOL.	R.K.9.
LE PREOL	5.8.16	10.0am	24th Brigade relieved in CUINCHY SECTION. 3 Guns taken into line. Battery H.Q. at ANNEQUIN. R.E.9.	R.K.9.
CUINCHY	6.8.16		H.Q. transferred to LE PREOL. Additional gun put in position. Ranges checked and fire observed. Quiet day except of enemy. Weather fine.	R.K.9.
"	7.8.16		2 more guns taken into line. Matching 6 Guns in all. 5 Farris trench gun positioned. Mine exploded by us at A.24.a.9.1. at 8.30pm. 2 Farris barrages on enemy trenches.	R.K.9.
"	8.8.16		Enemy retaliation to our fire cancelled. Our guns kept up fire of 2 to 1 of enemy.	R.K.9.
"	9.8.16		Positions for 3 new emplacements chosen and work commenced by R.E. Quiet day except for sniping in BRICKSTACKS about about 7.30 a.m. Weather fine except about 7.30a.m.	R.K.9.
"	10.8.16		Quiet Period. 1st Dorset Rift.	R.K.9.
"	11.8.16		2/Lieut. F.C. SQUIRES joined for duty.	R.K.9.
"	12.8.16		Quiet period. Weather hot.	R.K.9.
"	13.8.16		Guns Harrassived. Guns very active on whole front.	R.K.9.
"	14.8.16		Enemy shelled BRICKSTACKS position; no retaliation in this quarter.	R.K.9.
"	15.8.16		Quiet period.	R.K.9.
"	16.8.16		Quiet. Infantry relief.	R.K.9.
"	17.8.16		Quiet. Enfilading as first. Light retaliation to our mortar fire.	R.K.9.

Army Form C. 2118

WAR DIARY
or
INTELLIGENCE SUMMARY
(Erase heading not required.)

14th T.M. Battery

Instructions regarding War Diaries and Intelligence Summaries are contained in F.S. Regs., Part II. and the Staff Manual respectively. Title Pages will be prepared in manuscript.

Place	Date	Hour	Summary of Events and Information	Remarks and references to Appendices
CUINCHY	Aug 18th		Quiet. Wet. Trenches bad.	R.L.G.
	19th		Our mortars active; enemy retaliated feebly but is still superior with his heavy mortars.	R.L.G.
	20th		At 5 p.m. had a combined shoot with 2" for 10 mins. Enemy retaliated slightly.	R.L.G.
	21st		Cut 4 p.m. bombarded with Stokes and 2" rapid fire. Very effective, many bombs dropping into trenches and some effective air bursts.	R.L.G.
	22nd		Combined shoot with 18 pdrs. and 2" at 3 p.m.	R.L.G.
	23rd		Quiet period. Infantry relief.	R.L.G.
	24th		Quiet.	R.L.G.
	25th		2 mines blown by us, one S. of IPSWICH CRATER and one S. of MIDNIGHT CRATER at 8.30 p.m. 2 of our guns took heavy pt on enemy front line behind new craters.	R.L.G.
	26th		Quiet.	R.L.G.
	27th		Our guns very active in spite of considerable retaliation by enemy.	R.L.G.
	28th		Quiet except for normal activity of mortars.	R.L.G.
	29th		Infantry relieved. Enemy artillery and mortars active about 4.30 p.m. by railway at point B30 ours at B3/32. with bursts of rapid fire.	R.L.G.
	30th		Enemy mortars searched for our position in N/W subsection. Much damage to trenches but our position untouched. We retaliated on enemy trenches A.22.a.30.65-65.65	R.L.G.
	31st		Enemy mortars particularly quiet in spite of our fire.	R.L.G.

R.L. George 2/Lieut.

7(a).

7. Should O.C. 'A' Coy. consider the wire in front of the objective of this Battalion sufficiently broken to allow of a gap being easily made, he will change his direction on to this point, and making gap, will carry out the attack as above — Each Coy. conforming to this new movement and also with the time table of barrage as detailed in Appendix B.1.

www.ingramcontent.com/pod-product-compliance
Lightning Source LLC
Chambersburg PA
CBHW081249170426
43191CB00037B/2093